Library of Congress Number: 73-12190   ISBN: O-87191-259-7

Published by Creative Education, Mankato, Minnesota 56001
Distributed by Childrens Press, 1224 West Van Buren Street, Chicago, Illinois 60607

Library of Congress Cataloging in Publication Data
Deegan, Paul J   1937-
    Jack Nicklaus, the golden bear.
    SUMMARY: A biography of the professional golfer who is one of only four who have won the Masters, the two Opens, and the PGA during a career.
    1. Nicklaus, Jack—Juvenile literature.
[1. Nicklaus, Jack.   2. Golf—Biography] I. Nelson, John, 1928-   illus. II. Title.
GV964.N5D43 796.352'092'4 [B] [92]
ISBN 0-87191-259-7 73-12190

jack
nicklaus
THE GOLDEN BEAR

By Paul Deegan

Illustrated By John Nelson

The husky blond golfer addressed the ball for a moment. Jack Nicklaus then moved into his powerful swing. The pleasant sound of wood smacking the golf ball hung in the air. The ball itself was becoming smaller against the blue sky. It landed near the middle of the fairway and rolled to a stop. The ball was over 300 yards from the tee.

The man who hit the shot is probably the best golfer ever. This day Jack Nicklaus (pronounced NICK-lus) was playing in the first round of a professional golf tournament. The place was the Westchester Country Club in suburban New York City. The winner of the Westchester Classic would receive $50,000. The champion would earn more money in four days than many people make in several years.

Jack was still about 170 yards away from the green on the third hole after his long tee shot. Jack had walked up the fairway and was selecting a club for his approach shot on this 500-yard-long hole. He chose a 4-iron after looking over the shot. He brought the club down swiftly and the ball headed in a low arc toward the green. The ball came down just short of the putting surface. The spin on the ball and the short grass halted it there.

A pitching wedge was Jack's club choice for his third shot on this par-5 hole. He took a short swing after carefully lining up his shot. The ball lit on the green a few feet from the cup. It rolled toward the hole and dropped in the cup.

Jack had played one of the longest holes on the Westchester course in 3 strokes. He had an eagle or 2 under par. Professional golfers often make birdies or one under pars. Eagles though come hard even for these super golfers.

Jack played well throughout the rest of his round. He finished the day with a 65. This was 7-under-par for the 18 holes. But that wasn't good enough for first place at the end of the first day. Another golfer had an even better first day round of 64.

Two days later the fourth and final round was at hand. Jack now had a 2-stroke lead. Nicklaus looked cool and relaxed this day, the press noted. He played that way too. He birdied three par 5 holes by two-put-

John Nelson

ting them. He played the final round in 68 strokes to win the Westchester Classic.

His score for the tournament was 270. This was 3 strokes better than any other player. The man who had led Nicklaus after one day had later fallen off the pace. Jack was 18 under par for four days of golf under pressure. Jack called his final round one of the best he'd ever played.

This late summer victory came past the midpoint of the annual professional golf tour. The season begins early in January in Los Angeles. It finishes 12 months later in Florida. Some pro golfers have to play in almost every tournament. Actually there are more golfers than spots in each tournament. So some of the golfers must qualify for each tournament if they can. They keep hoping that they will break into that group of golfers who make money playing the game.

Jack Nicklaus leads this group. He is the only golfer who has won over $2 million. This is only his official prize winnings. He won thousands more in other tournaments which were not part of the regular tour. Jack wins more often than anyone now playing golf. He has won over 45 tournaments in his 14 years of professional golf.

One of these victories came on a warm December day in Florida. At this time of year many golf courses in the north were covered with snow. Some pro football teams were playing in near zero temperatures. But the sun was shining brightly for the final round of the Walt

Disney World Open Golf tournament. This was the final tournament on the 1972 PGA (Professional Golfers Association) tour.

Nicklaus had more at stake than winning another tournament. If he won, he would be the first golfer ever to win more than $300,000 in official prize money

in one year. He had already passed Arnold Palmer as the leading money winner in golf.

Jack was 9 under par after the first 54 holes of the Disney tournament. He was leading the field by 2 strokes. Nicklaus has often been described as a great competitor. He was this day. He shot a 64 on the final 18 holes. It was his best round of the tournament. His 8-under-par round left him way in front. Three men finished in a tie for second. They weren't even close. Jack beat them by 9 strokes.

Jack's total score for the Disney tournament was 267. This was the best score made by any professional player in the entire season. The victory was his seventh win for the year. No golfer had won that many tournaments in one year since 1960 when Arnold Palmer won 8.

The one-year money record set by Nicklaus came about because he usually finished near the top if he did not win a tournament. Nicklaus entered less than half of the tournaments on the 1972 PGA tour. He was among the top 10 finishers in 15 of the 20 tournaments he entered.

Nicklaus was the top money-winner in golf in 6 of his first 13 years on the tour. The amount of money offered on the pro tour increases each year. Television is the most important factor in this regard. The total money now offered on the pro tour is 10 times greater than it was 25 years ago. Nicklaus in 1973 again won over $300,000 in one year.

Golf and making a fantastic amount of money were not Jack's childhood dreams. His father, Charles, was a successful drug store owner in Columbus, Ohio. As a youngster, Jack didn't have to be concerned about money. He did like sports though. He spent much of his free time playing baseball, football, and basketball, depending upon the season.

Jack first went on the golf course when he was 10. Maybe he wouldn't have played golf until much later if his father hadn't injured his ankle. The injury resulted in an operation. While recovering from the operation, his father couldn't keep up with his fellow golfers. He had to stop and rest after playing a couple of holes. Rather than play by himself, he took Jack along.

The first time Jack played 9 holes, he shot a 51. His father played at Scioto Country Club in Columbus. A new golf instructor had been hired by the club. He gave group lessons to Jack and other junior members. His father also arranged for Jack to have private lessons every so often. Using a cut-down set of clubs, Jack began playing a lot of golf. Before that first summer was over, Jack shot a 95 for 18 holes on the difficult Scioto course.

The following summer Jack continued taking lessons from Jack Grout, the Scioto golf pro. Grout encouraged his young students to develop a big swing. Today Nicklaus consistently outhits his fellow professionals. He regularly drives the ball over 300 yards off the tee. This is 25 to 50 yards farther than most other players. Jack also gets a lot of distance on his iron shots. He is able to make some greens in 2 strokes while others need 3 shots to cover the same distance.

Grout also encouraged Jack to hit his iron shots high. This gives the ball more bite when it lands. A shot hit to where you want it quickly becomes a bad shot if the ball doesn't stay put. Grout also taught Jack to hit his woods and long iron shots so that the ball went from left to right in flight. This is known as a fade. Using this skill, Jack can control his shot in almost every situation.

Jack Grout is the only golf teacher that Jack Nicklaus has ever had. Grout has left Columbus and

is now a pro in Miami Beach, Florida. Sometimes even Jack Nicklaus still has trouble with his golf game. In 1973, Jack came to Miami Beach, went to Grout, hit one ball to check if he had corrected a problem in his swing, and flew back to Ohio.

The young Nicklaus had the benefit of Grout's constant guidance. When he was 11, Jack got his first set of full-sized clubs. That year he shot an 81 to qualify for a local tournament. The future professional champi-

on was beaten in his first tournament by a 13-year-old.

The next few summers found Jack continuing to spend much of his time on the golf course. His improvement continued. He broke 70 for the first time when he was 13. His first under-70 round began at Scioto late one afternoon after his father came home from his stores. Before this day, Jack's best round had been a 2-over-par 74.

After shooting a 34 on the first 9 holes, Jack was anxious to keep going. He wanted to see if he could break into the 60's for the first time. Jack also feared that it would be too dark to finish 18 holes if they took time to eat. However, his father said that his mother was waiting dinner. So home they went.

The Nicklaus home was very near the Scioto course. Father and son hustled home and gulped their meal. They rushed back to the course. By the time Jack finished the 17th hole, his chances for breaking 70

seemed slim. He needed an eagle 3 on the 18th hole. The 18th at Scioto is a long par-five. It was now also almost dark.

Jack hit a good drive on 18. When he ran to his ball, he found he had a problem. It was so dark that he couldn't see the flag on the green. He could see a sprinkler on the green that the groundskeepers had already turned on. Jack knew he needed a very

good shot. He selected a 2-iron and aimed for the sprinkler.

He hurried to the green and found the ball 35 feet from the cup. The putting surface was wet. Years later, Jack was to be in similar tough situations. The green would be wet with rain. Fame and money would then be riding on the putt. The only thing involved this time was achieving a personal goal. Jack struck the putt and the ball rolled over the soggy turf. Plop! It dropped in the cup. Jack had an eagle-three on 18, a 35 on the back 9, and an 18-hole total of 69.

That summer Jack played in more tournaments. He won the Ohio tournament for boys 13 to 15. He played in his first national tournament, winning his first three matches at the Southern Hills course in Tulsa, Oklahoma.

The next summer, when he was 14, Jack played on his high school golf team. He also took part in a national boys tournament in Los Angeles. That year also saw him score his first hole-in-one.

As a 15-year-old, he continued to win local tournaments for teenagers. He also qualified for the first time for the United States Amateur tournament. The tournament was played that year in Richmond, Virginia. Most of the other golfers were men several years older than Jack. Jack lost in the first round.

It was during this U.S. Amateur that Jack first met Bobby Jones, his golfing hero. Bobby Jones—Robert T. Jones Jr.—was one of the great golfers of all time.

He was one of the sports heroes of the 1920's. Jones always remained an amateur golfer. He never played golf for money. One of the many tournaments Jones won was at Scioto in Columbus. That was the 1926 United States Open.

Jack's father was a teenager in 1926. He and his friends saw Jones play at Scioto. Later these men realized that Jack was going to be a good golfer. They tried to inspire him by telling him about Jones. They talked about the tournament where they saw Jones 14 years before Jack was born.

Now Nicklaus and Jones came together for the first time. Jones was watching while Jack played a practice round before the Amateur in Richmond. Jones could see how much natural ability the young golfer had. He asked to meet Jack. After that first meeting, the two became friends. Until Jones died in 1971, they got together each spring when Jack went to Augusta, Georgia, for the Masters tournament. Jones started the Masters and helped design the Augusta National course.

Jack returned home from Richmond determined to improve his game. The next summer he won his

most important victory as a boy. Then 16 years old, he beat the top golfers from throughout the state of Ohio to win the Ohio State Open. He shot a remarkable 64 in the third round of this tournament.

The following year, Nicklaus qualified for the U.S. Open tournament for the first time. He was 17 and just out of high school. The 1957 Open was played at Inverness. Bobby Jones played in his first U.S. Open when it too was at Inverness. Jones had been 18.

Jack did not play well enough to make the final rounds of the 1957 Open. But he was entering more important tournaments and learning a good deal about himself and his game. He was discovering how to make shots that not only looked good but also kept his score down. He was learning to play similar shots differently depending upon the situation. His score and whether or not he was leading became more important when he was deciding how he wanted to play the ball. Playing on many courses, often difficult ones, helped develop his game.

Jack has said that he didn't begin taking golf seriously until just before graduating from high school. However, he had given up football and track when he started at Upper Arlington high in suburban Columbus. As a boy, Jack liked sandlot baseball and played on his junior high school football and track teams. He quarterbacked the football team when he was in 8th grade. He scored 3 touchdowns and kicked 6 extra points in his team's final game that year.

Jack was kidded often about being fat when he began playing professional golf. Yet he was a sprinter and high jumper on his junior high track team. But football and track cut into the golf season, so Jack dropped them in high school. Even so, basketball, not golf, was his favorite sport in high school. He and 3 classmates started on the Upper Arlington varsity team for 3 years. A husky 6-footer, Jack averaged nearly 18 points a game during his 2nd and 3rd years as a starter. He was all-conference as a senior.

Several colleges offered Jack scholarships to play golf at their schools. He turned them all down to go to school in his hometown. He did not receive a golf scholarship at Ohio State. Golf was a sport he loved. He did not consider it as a way to make his living. Jack was thinking about working with his father and took pre-pharmacy courses at Ohio State.

Jack started college in the fall of 1957. Golf was now more important to him than even basketball. One of the reasons he chose golf over other sports was that he could practice and play golf alone. He also felt golf was a big challenge. It demanded much study and constant practice.

Snow and cold weather come to Ohio in the winter. But this weather didn't stop Jack from practicing golf. There was a small driving range in the Nicklaus basement. Jack could also hit balls at Scioto where Jack Grout came up with a way to beat the long winters. The pro had a large hut put up. One side was open to a practice fairway. The hut was heated with a stove. Nicklaus spent many winter hours hitting balls from the hut.

Jack didn't need too much time to get ready for golf matches when good weather came. The summer after his first year at Ohio State saw Jack make it to the final round of the U.S. Amateur tournament. The Amateur was played in San Francisco that year. Jack was 18 and playing against the best non-professional golfers in the world. He lost in match play on the final hole.

Some major tournaments were once match play. One golfer plays against another and the loser is out. The number of holes won determines the winner. Total strokes do not. Match play is often exciting but all major tournaments are now stroke play.

This is due to television. People who televise sports and the companies that pay for the televising don't like match play. A well-known golfer such as Nicklaus can be beaten early in the tournament. He won't be playing when the final rounds are televised. Those in television believe that people at home won't watch tournament golf if the big names are missing. Companies buying the advertising which pays for televising sports events want as many people watching as possible. So all major tournaments are now stroke play where a golfer can have a bad early round and still be a contender on the final day.

Jack also played in his first PGA tour event when he was 18. He finished 12th in the Rubber City Open at Akron, Ohio. Jack continued winning amateur tournaments throughout the country.

The next summer Jack Nicklaus' name began to appear in sports pages all over the United States. He won his first major golf championship and he played in Scotland, the country where golf was first played.

First came the trip to Scotland. Jack had been chosen to play on the United States Walker Cup team. Every two years, the best amateur players from the United States and Great Britain play each other. The 1959 match was to be held at Muirfield.

In Britain, people are not as casual about golf as in this country. Everything about golf was once very formal in Britain. The official name of the course at Muirfield, for instance, is The Honourable Company of Edinburgh Golfers, Muirfield. Even the golf ball used in Britain is different. It is slightly smaller. In his first trip abroad, Jack won his matches as the United States team easily took the Walker Cup. It was the United States' 18th win in 19 Walker Cup matches.

Later that summer, Jack faced a Walker Cup teammate in the final match of the U.S. Amateur. Jack beat Charlie Coe at Colorado Springs, Colorado, to win his first major championship.

The following summer centered around something other than golf. Jack married Barbara Bash, a fellow student at Ohio State. She is also from Columbus. The new Mrs. Nicklaus found out right away how much Jack liked golf. He spent part of their honeymoon playing some famous golf courses in the eastern states. He got to play on these private courses because he was becoming known as one of the best golfers in the country.

Several weeks before his marriage, Jack made the 36-hole cut in the Masters for the first time. Playing well in the Masters has always been important to Nicklaus because of his friendship with Bobby Jones. This time he tied for low amateur in the Masters.

Later that summer Jack came close to winning the U.S. Open. Playing at Cherry Hills in Denver,

Colorado, Jack was leading with only six holes to play. But Arnold Palmer won. Jack was second. Palmer was then the top winner and most popular player in professional golf. Palmer won seven more tournaments that summer, a record that Jack almost broke in 1972. Palmer was Jack's biggest rival during the 1960's after Jack became a professional.

But at 20, Jack was still an amateur. Before he was 21, sportswriters were calling Nicklaus the greatest amateur since Bobby Jones. This came after his sensational play in the World Amateur Team Championships. Thirty-two countries sent teams to Merion in a Philadelphia suburb. Jack has said that Merion is one of the finest golf courses in this country. He has also said that great golf courses inspire him. He was inspired at Merion in 1960.

Nicklaus set a course record for amateurs in his first round. He shot a 66. He had a 67 the second day and finished with two rounds of 68. The United States team won easily. Jack finished 13 strokes ahead of the field.

Jack had established himself as one of the best golfers in the world. Yet he still wasn't seriously considering professional golf. He did change his studies at Ohio State from pharmacy to business and began selling insurance. He combined golf with his marriage, his school work, and his business. During his last two years at Ohio State he played on the university golf team.

Jack was the medalist—he had the best score—in both the 1961 conference and national college championship tournaments. These were played in the spring of his final year at Ohio State. That summer he won his second U.S. Amateur championship. That fall, Barb and Jack's first child, Jack Nicklaus III, was born.

Jack was still undecided about his future. His insurance business was doing well. He talked to Bobby Jones about playing professional golf. He met with a man whose business was making money for famous athletes. These athletes are paid for letting their names be used to advertise many things, including sports equipment and clothes. Jack was told that he could make $100,000 if he became a professional. This would be

in addition to whatever he won playing golf.

Jack continued to think about what he wanted to do with his life. He considered golf a game rather than a business. Even so, he had to wonder how he would do playing against the best golfers week after week. As a professional, he would play on the most famous courses in the world. He finally decided to become a professional golfer.

He made this decision late in 1961. His first year on the pro tour was 1962. He entered 26 tournaments and won some money in each of them. Sometimes it wasn't very much. He won only $33 in his first tournament. But by the end of his first year as a pro golfer, Nicklaus had won almost $62,000. The highlight of the first year was a victory in the U.S. Open. He beat Arnold Palmer in a playoff.

The Open victory was Jack's third major tournament win, his first as a professional. As a pro golfer he would no longer be able to play in the U.S. Amateur, which he had won twice. The Amateur and four other tournaments held each year are considered the major tournaments. The others are the Masters, the U.S. Open, the PGA, and the British Open.

In the next 11 years Jack was to win 11 more times in these tournaments. He won the PGA in 1963, 1971, and 1973. He took the British Open in 1966 and 1970. He won two more U.S. Opens—1967 and 1972. He won the Masters four times—1963, 1965, 1966, and 1972.

Jack has won more major tournaments, 14, than any other golfer. His boyhood hero, Bobby Jones, had won 13. Nicklaus got his 14th major win in August 1973. The event was the 1973 PGA played in suburban Cleveland, Ohio. Nicklaus was 7 under par for the tournament played on the tough Canterbury Country Club course. He won by 4 strokes.

Nine of the major tournament wins came by the time Nicklaus was 27. He then went over 2 years before he won another. His 10th win came in Scotland in the 1970 British Open. The tournament was played on The Old Course at St. Andrews. This course is hundreds of years old. It is said to be the place where golf was born. Jack has strong feelings for golf's traditions. Winning the Open at St. Andrews made him feel a part of golf's history.

Jack's first British Open win came at Muirfield in 1966. He had played in the Walker Cup match there 7 years earlier. With the 1966 victory at Muirfield, Jack became only the fourth golfer to win the Masters, the two Opens, and the PGA during a career. Winning all four of them in the same year is known as the "Grand Slam" of golf. Nobody has ever done this. After topping Jones' record, winning the "Grand Slam" is Jack's biggest goal.

He had a chance for the "Grand Slam" in 1972.

He won the Masters and the U.S. Open before going back to Scotland for the British Open. The tournament was again being played at Muirfield. Jack got off to a bad start. Going into the final day, he was six strokes behind the leader, Lee Trevino. But Jack is a competitor. Jack Grout, the man who taught him to play golf, has said this is a major reason for Nicklaus' success. Jack tied the course record on the final round. He did this on perhaps Scotland's best golf course. His closing 66, though, was not quite enough to win. Trevino won by one stroke. Jack's try for the "Grand Slam" had to be put off for another year.

Nicklaus is not only today's leading golfer. He is also a very successful businessman. He heads a company called Golden Bear, Inc. Jack was nicknamed the "Golden Bear" before he went on a diet a couple of years ago. He had decided that the extra weight was hurting his golf game. Jack lost 20 pounds and gave himself a new image. He looked as if he'd lost much more than 20 pounds. His clothes appeared to hang on him before. Now they looked sharp. He also let his hair grow longer and threw away his golf hats. The fans at a tournament or watching TV now get a closer look at a jaunty Jack Nicklaus moving over a golf course.

The new image made him an even more popular subject for advertisers. About the same time that Jack changed his appearance, he became his own business manager. Jack's company is involved in many things.

He advertises cars and has an auto dealership. The company also builds golf courses. Jack himself helps design these courses. He really likes the golf courses in Scotland. He put some of the special features found on Scottish courses into the new ones. One of these is in his hometown of Columbus. It is called the Muirfield Village Golf Club. The name is taken from the course in Scotland where Jack won the 1966 British Open. The Ohio course is designed for major tournament play.

Despite his success in golf and business, Jack is still able to spend a good deal of time with his family. This is one reason he only plays in about half the tournaments on the pro tour.

Jack, Barb, and their five children live in a huge house near Palm Beach, Florida. The house is next to Lake Worth. There is a grass tennis court on the Nicklaus property. Jack plays tennis often when he's home.

Jack also owns an ocean-going fishing boat. He has taken the boat to the Bahama Islands, where he has a vacation place. Fishing is one of his favorite ways to relax. He also plays ball and bowls with the children.

There is time, too, for watching the oldest boys—Jack, now a teenager, and Steve, 11—play on neighborhood teams. Young Jack scores well on the golf course. Sometimes he accompanies his father during practice rounds on the pro tour. Nancy, 9, is the only Nicklaus daughter. Gary is 6 and Michael is 2.

There are those who say that Jack spends so much time away from golf that his game will suffer. Nicklaus doesn't agree. So far he has been able to live as many people wish they could. He makes a great deal of money in golf and in business and loves both the game and his work. He can also spend a lot more time with the people he loves. Jack Nicklaus probably would not trade places with anybody else in the whole world.

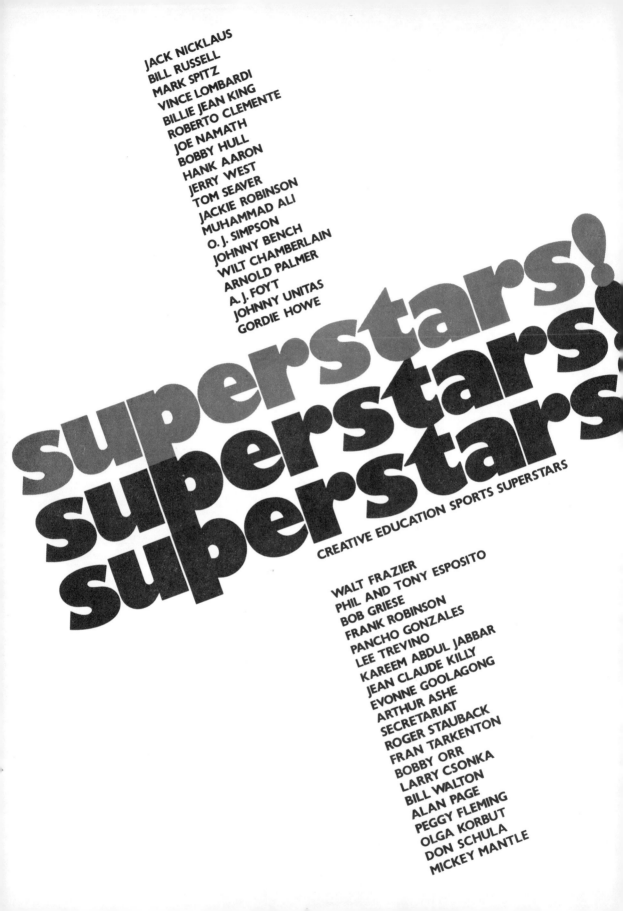

JACK NICKLAUS
BILL RUSSELL
MARK SPITZ
VINCE LOMBARDI
BILLIE JEAN KING
ROBERTO CLEMENTE
JOE NAMATH
BOBBY HULL
HANK AARON
JERRY WEST
TOM SEAVER
JACKIE ROBINSON
MUHAMMAD ALI
O. J. SIMPSON
JOHNNY BENCH
WILT CHAMBERLAIN
ARNOLD PALMER
A. J. FOYT
JOHNNY UNITAS
GORDIE HOWE

superstars!
superstars!
superstars!
superstars!

CREATIVE EDUCATION SPORTS SUPERSTARS

WALT FRAZIER
PHIL AND TONY ESPOSITO
BOB GRIESE
FRANK ROBINSON
PANCHO GONZALES
LEE TREVINO
KAREEM ABDUL JABBAR
JEAN CLAUDE KILLY
EVONNE GOOLAGONG
ARTHUR ASHE
SECRETARIAT
ROGER STAUBACK
FRAN TARKENTON
BOBBY ORR
LARRY CSONKA
BILL WALTON
ALAN PAGE
PEGGY FLEMING
OLGA KORBUT
DON SCHULA
MICKEY MANTLE

/